M000219008

poems for the signs

michaela angemeer

poems for the signs copyright © 2022 by Michaela Angemeer. No part of this book may be used or reproduced in any manner whatsoever without written permission except in the case of reprints in the context of reviews.

michaelapoetry.com

Artwork by Michaela Angemeer

ISBN: 978-1-7752727-4-8

*for dad and your enthusiasm
in discovering the unknown*

i know we just met but
send me your birth time

table of contents

preface

i've never written a preface for my books before, so i am very
excited for this. hi, it's me, michaela. i thought before you read
a book with my interpretation of the astrological signs, i should
give you a little explanation so you don't get mad at me.

my love for astrology started at a young age, as soon as i found
out i was a scorpio sun. that's why i love death and darkness so
much? i felt seen. finding out i wasn't just rude for fun and that it
was my sagittarius mercury? huge. fast forward twenty years and
i'm now the friend that knows everyone's sun signs. and if i've
gotten your birth time out of you, i definitely remember at least
your big three.

i love using astrology as a tool for self-reflection. i love seeing
the beautiful ways that certain placements show up in people's
lives. by more deeply studying astrology over the past few years,
i've learned to make less assumptions based on placements and
ask more questions. the ways in which people's charts actualize
can be so unique when you add layers of houses, degrees, and
aspects, the experiences they've had and the amount of self-
reflection they've done. i see astrology as an opportunity to learn
about people vs. a way to make a snap judgment.

these poems were lovingly written and inspired by so many
things. some of them were written about people with certain
placements that stick out to me. some of them made their way
into a certain sign because of the energy they hold. some of them
were written as love letters for specific signs based on what i
think people in my life, past and present, need to hear. many of
the poems, no matter the section they're in, are things we all (me
included) need to hear more often.

like all my books, there are some brutally honest takes in these poems. but if you're reading a section about a placement you have, i just want you to know it doesn't mean i think all people with that sun sign are that way, or that people with placements in that sign need to learn that lesson. it just resonated with me and the experiences i've had.

i hope you find love in each section, no matter what your sun sign is or what placements you have in your chart. we all have aspects of the twelve signs in us, even if we don't have specific placements. i hope this collection makes you and all your parts feel loved.

xoxo
m

how to read

hello earth placements, i know you're mainly the ones reading this.

if you're new to astrology, or maybe are just familiar with sun signs (also known as zodiac signs–based on birthdays), feel free to read your sign first. you can also easily find the sun sign of people in your life if you know their birthday, whether it's your partner, family, friend, or let's be real, your ex.

if you want to go a little deeper and read the poems for your major placements (which are sun, moon, ascendant, mercury, mars, and venus) and you don't know them already, i recommend using astro.com to find your birth chart. you'll need your birth time to do this. if you've used other popular apps to find your chart already, it's worth mentioning that they often miscalculate ascendants (also known as your rising sign) and moon signs. so as a bossy virgo moon, i'm telling you, astro.com is the most accurate.

the collection also reads well if you start with aries (the first sign of the zodiac) and end with pisces (the last sign), in my humble opinion. astrology aside, it's a collection about looking for love, self-reflection, healing ancestral patterns, and finding beauty in being alone.

p.s. now that i've written all this, i realize that 'how to read' is a misnomer. i've given you about ten options. i am a gemini rising, what can i say.

aries

[air-eez]
noun

1. the first sign of the zodiac: the cardinal fire sign
2. a person born under this sign, usually between march 21 and april 19

the hare
plant fertilizer
bungee jumping off a shaky bridge
lost carnelian
new velcro shoes
starting a fire with damp newspaper
birthday money without a card
a golden retriever with no collar
making friends on a plane
are we there yet?
flintstone
max volume

aries

i'm finally starting to learn
that who can do the hurt first
without getting hurt in return
isn't a competition i want to win

i am a bathtub filled with boiling water
tic-tac-toe in red crayon on a restaurant table
mom doesn't let me win
itching the rash on the small of my back
eating frosted flakes from the box
sugar stuck in my nails
crusty morning eyes that won't wipe off
they say you should never
paint your kitchen red
cause it makes you hungry
lying drunk on the sidewalk
i told you i loved you
but then i forgot
dad talks to opa's ghost in the river
what will happen to our bloodline
mom closed the gap between her teeth
my womb wonders
will i ever be filled

are you in love or
are you just scared
of being alone

i thought i was self aware
before i even knew
how i was feeling
about anything other
than someone else

falling in love is
cloud nine
dancing in your underwear
good morning texts
giving someone the ability
to make you cry

i know we know
this is better for both of us
i know no love was lost
and trees can't grow
when they're planted so close
but sometimes it's sad
to lose your person

sometimes it's sad to be alone

you are already the flame. stop looking for matchsticks. think bigger. your energy is a gift. most people can't see the finish line before they've started the race, but you can. harness your power. the people who tell you you're too big have spent their whole lives afraid to grow. if someone makes you feel like shrinking, leave them. if someone tells you to give up, push harder. you owe it to yourself to fill up this world with passion and love in a way that only you can.

it took me twenty-seven years
to learn how to lie
i thought honesty
was a natural inclination
for everyone
i know that's sweet
i love the person i used to be
but unfortunately
i also loved a lot of liars
who knew the lies
that would work on me

i don't wanna be with anybody
who weaponizes my vulnerability
saves it in a wooden box
loads it in a shotgun
when i least expect it

what if you stopped looking at
the people who don't love you
what if you turned towards
all the ones who do

you are divinely held
you have already survived
your most difficult moments
you will survive what's to come
the universe wants to help

all you need to do is surrender

some days being alone feels like the worst thing in the world but some days it's not that bad. some days it's staying in bed to feel the warmth of my sheets a little longer. some days it's eggs benedict and a matcha latte. some days it's a crisp walk in the cemetery. some days it's a perfectly clear sky. some days it's reading books that change my life. some days it's writing something that changes my perspective. some days it's antique shopping and finding something hidden. some days it's a car ride with my favourite album from when i was a kid. some days it's puppy snuggles and a movie. some days it's feeling like this is who i was meant to be. some days there is no one i would rather be with than me.

one day, i promise
there will be someone you can let in
who will keep you safe once they're inside

taurus

[tawr-uhs]
noun

1. the second sign of the zodiac: the fixed earth sign
2. a person born under this sign, usually between april 20 and may 20

the tortoise
cinnamon buns
a hug after two years
the last two minutes of a vanilla-scented candle
an old t-shirt
munchies at midnight
not taking advice
inertia
a forest nymph
worn-in work boots on the front porch
sharpening a pencil to the last inch
your childhood best friend's phone number

taurus

is it mercury retrograde
or would i still miss you either way

i thought i would always love you
but while i was standing in the sun
you kept looking for shade
the more i nourished
the more you withered
i tried to make us last longer
emptied my cup
to fill up yours
until i learned that
there's no point in watering
something that doesn't want to grow

33

all the planets are direct
so i can't use retrograde
as an excuse for why i'm depressed
haven't showered in two days
or left the house
and the only question
i can seem to answer is
how can i make myself
feel more numb

it's ok to go slow
all that matters
is that you're in flow

i grew up sitting on the edge
of your waterbed
never punctured
so how could i know
that it wasn't filled with water
it was a whirlpool
of your spinning third eye
and sixty-six years of wanting
a hopeful heart
but painting the mirror black instead
thirty-one years of crocheting it into a blanket
handed down to me
i put it in the trunk of my car
drove around with knit unworthiness
and wondered why
i've always found it so hard
to stitch myself together
even though i have all the parts

you have blessed the earth
for ninety-five years
with wit and wisdom
on your heels
why can't you see all
the seeds you've planted
why can't you see
i watered them
why can't you see

i turned everything into love for you

the greatest love story ever told
was not between lovers
but soulmates
brought together by their children
whose hearts had to go separate ways
luckily theirs remained
best friends beyond the grave
and still to this day
i've never seen love like
how my oma loved my nana
and she loved her right back

you hold the pulse of the earth in your hands. your stability is a superpower. you've witnessed tornados, earthquakes, tsunamis and hurricanes, but still you stand strong. keep going at your own pace. say no to anyone who wants you to rush. they may think they know better, but they'll stop long before you. listen to the trees. the flowers have secrets for you. the more you connect with the earth, the more purpose you'll feel. if you ever feel lost or discouraged, plant your bare feet on the ground. wait. the answer will come.

i surrender to wealth
i surrender to success
i surrender to divine timing
i surrender to all the gifts
the universe will gladly give me

you may never let go completely
but you will move on

you can set boundaries with people. you can say all the right things. and still, some patterns of abuse are too powerful to break. still, your inner child knows that when you walk into a room with them, you are not safe. they can brush it off as an innocent slip up and you can too. but ask yourself, if it was your child, would you let them be around a person who has slip ups? would you let them be around someone who chips away at their self worth? even for a second? for me, the answer was no. and as much as it hurts, my inner child thanks me every day for keeping us safe. for taking us out of a situation where we felt scared and helpless. and for becoming the parent we never had.

i just want to feel safe enough
to fall in love

you'll find me in the meadow
tangled hair bits of grass
i've plucked all the wildflowers
now they sing your name
while i wail it
toes caked in mud
fistfuls of twigs
i found a morel by a fallen tree
red jasper in the marsh
wade through the river
could you hear me scream?
i thought i lost my voice
i mean
i only spoke the truth through shattered teeth
but you are honey-coated throat
i thought i lost my way
i mean
i burned all the maps they gave me
but then i heard you coming

gemini

[jem-uh-nahy]
noun

1. the third sign of the zodiac: the mutable air sign
2. a person born under this sign, usually between may 21 and june 20

losing your fake ID
wishing on a dandelion
arguing without caring if you're right
a glass table with a scratch
flipping a coin
not knowing how to keep a secret
an old bullet journal completely filled in
a mirrorball
howlite under the pillow
inflatable furniture
three shots of tequila
a voice crack

gemini

is this the line for lobotomies
i'd love one
i told you to stop thinking
but you came up with more words instead
what is it like to feel peace?
i've lived a lifelong civil war
the battlefield is my frontal lobe
and no one ever wins

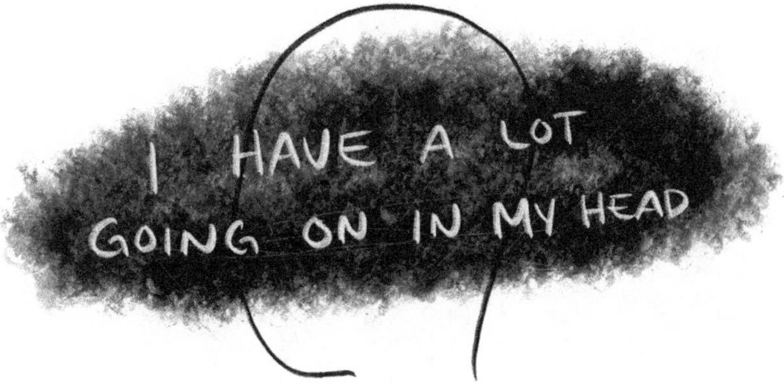
I HAVE A LOT
GOING ON IN MY HEAD

i kept dating in the hopes
that someone else's body
would keep me warm
but all i got was cold feet

have you ever noticed you're incredible?
even just for a second
or have you always held it in
scared of taking your own breath away
but there is joy
in this kind of love for self
not egoistic
or narcissistic
seeing both sides of the coin
and not caring which one it lands on
because you like both
and you are both
you are the beginning
the in-between
and the ending
and the only thing more heartbreaking
than no one else acknowledging it
is that they taught you
to ignore it too

i have been programmed
by the stars
and my mother
to see the worst in things

you can understand
where someone is coming from
and still not accept how they treat you

i yearn for all my
former best friends
talking about our periods at recess

first crushes
first kisses
first i-think-i-love-somebodys

i miss french braids
and reading cosmo before we knew
what anything really meant

there's something about friendship
that gives you hope for your future
a sibling by choice

but sometimes it doesn't rain for weeks
sometimes you move to new cities
you become new people

and when you come home
you realize the river you used to
walk in together has evaporated

i can't name
all the people i've been
since i was a kid

almost drowning in nana's pool
getting lost at a polkaroo concert
boys can like pink
chapstick at recess
crushes liking my best friend
mom editing everything in red pen
don't do this to the kids
a german shepherd with anxiety
not suburban enough
talking back
first boyfriend in grade eight
hugging once not eating for days
women can't be pastors
seventeen my voice got louder
first kiss in a dirty bar
not saying yes but never really having a choice

what is reality
and what is part of the narrative
my anxiety invented

i wish i could remember
what sign the moon was in
when i told you
i loved you
i don't remember
if i said it cause
i was feeling bold
sad
or both

it's okay if most of the love in your twenties
was unrequited

it's okay if you spent more time pining
than being loved back

it's okay if you wanted love so badly
it terrified you

it's okay if it made the in-between easier
than the real thing

you are the magician. look, right here. your power is within. you don't need to keep searching for answers. put down the telescope. the stars are beautiful, but so is your heart. take a deep breath. count to ten. sometimes you can't think your way to the answer. sometimes you have to trust that you know the way. all you have to do is steer. follow your intuition. grace, joy, and peace are with you every day. just look inside yourself.

i am not a good person
or a bad person
my morality will never be black and white
my soul is a rainbow
you can make a million colours from it
and all of them are beautiful

cancer

[kan-ser]
noun

1. the fourth sign of the zodiac: the cardinal water sign
2. a person born under this sign, usually between june 21
and july 22

crying in gym class
a porcelain doll
forget-me-nots
wool mittens attached with a string
a perfectly timed punchline
feeling homesick
a car ride with silent understanding
floating in the ocean
an empty box of wine
have i ever told you i love you?
driving towards the moon
a crumpled up love letter

cancer

hush little baby
don't say a word
everyone doesn't hate you
the sky is just falling
and they're busy picking it up

i am too considerate of people i've never met

my inner child took me
to the ocean
jumped in the waves
watched the clouds
you miss me but i'm right here
she told me to hug trees
but i got a rash
and an inchworm in my cotton bra
she told me to be less serious
but i cried instead
and mourned the girl
she never got to be

i was raised on guilt and shame
i'm just trying to be myself again

take me where the water ends
i'm tired of being the only mermaid
you promised atlantis
but all i got was myrtle beach
and the sand is still stuck in my bottoms

i thought you said poseidon was on his way
instead i'm shooting tequila
from flamingo-shaped glasses
lick the salt from my shoulder
there are no limes underwater

we were the sea once
now you buy me boardwalk t-shirts and puka shells
while i'm dreaming of the heart of the ocean
pull the sun from my shoulders
i'm tap dancing with the undertow

don't make me ride the ferris wheel
we'll get stuck up there
i freed all the orcas
please let me swim with them

i don't belong here anymore
but you want me to be human
i don't belong to you
but you wouldn't have it any other way

truthfully,
i find it so difficult to know
who wants the real me
and who just wants to feel seen

sometimes we put wishes
onto people
that they aren't ready
to make come true

you can't build a home
out of red flags

my loneliness is a
coping mechanism
protection from rejection

why did i let you in
you can't practice vulnerability
on someone
who's never felt their feelings

why did i try to go deep
you weren't comfortable in my ocean
too many waves for someone
who never learned to swim

why didn't i see
that i was the one giving everything
and you were stuck inside yourself
too scared to be anything other than numb

sometimes the best thing you can do
for the people you love
is take care of yourself

you are not too much. you are brilliant. remarkable. you fill up rooms with love. you are joy. you are sunlight. you put more stars in the sky. your laugh makes the earth a better place. every day the world tells you to hide. but you say no. your soul was put here to take up as much space as possible. and there is room for you to be even more.

no matter how much
i love someone
i can say no to them
and they can say no to me
and i won't be abandoned
and i won't be rejected
and no love will be lost

leo

[lee-oh]
noun

1. the fifth sign of the zodiac: the fixed fire sign
2. a person born under this sign, usually between july 23 and august 22

a brazilian blowout
not asking for directions
a purple heart
acting single
breaking in shoes
the lead in your high school play
a ten-foot tall sunflower
the cheshire cat
sunburn on your nose
who would you be if you weren't afraid?
a dog jumping over a fence
sex on the beach

leo

what if you let the love stay
and let go of the rest

i am done with maybe loves
love is not for maybes
romeo didn't drink half the poison
juliet plunged the sword all the way in
it's time for full-fledged love
i deserve something definite

hiding from your feelings
doesn't make them go away
it covers them with black mud
bubbling up when you least expect it
spilling into everything
you hoped would feel good
until you can't feel anything at all

this time i didn't tell my friends
this time i didn't save your number
this time i didn't think about the future
this time i didn't cry
this time i felt nothing

your words were beautiful
but an empty promise
is just a lie that hurts more

you are allowed to be your full self. do not dim your light or change your identity for anyone. the weird parts of you, the things you feel shame around. they are beautiful and they are meant to be seen. the right people will find you. the right people will see your bravery. the right people will look at all the parts of you that you weren't sure about, and they'll adore them. pretending to be someone else will only make you feel empty. you deserve to be loved for who you are. there are so many blessings looking for you. and the only way they can find you is if you start to live your life for you.

i invited you
to join me in the woods
but the universe said *no*
find pleasure by yourself instead

if this is supposed to be
you still need your solitude
need nights alone
mornings where you wake up to
your own smile

she said, baby
i'll give you all the love
in the world
as long as you promise
to not abandon yourself again

being selfish isn't always a bad thing

i love you. please keep laughing and smiling and finding joy in the little things. you make life better. thank you for reminding me that not everything has to be so serious all the time. you are the definition of pure, unaltered love, and i love you so much for it. never stop dancing, singing, expressing yourself in whatever way feels right to you. you were put on this earth to be you. i know you have been hurt and put down, and for that i am sorry. i will never listen to anyone who tries to get you to dim your light again.

to my inner child

this is a reminder
of who you are
what you've been through
and how far you've come

i'm proud of you

the only thing that changed is i stopped waiting for a partner to live my life. bought myself flowers. took myself on dates. real dates. dressed up for fun. journaled in the park and enjoyed my own company. went on vacation. a three-hour drive for one. a three bedroom cottage for one. planned dinners. shucked corn. barbecued. lit candles. ate. did the dishes after. talked to mother mary in the lake. took pictures in the hot tub. lit incense every morning. practiced gratitude every night. read two books in two days. watched the sunset on the dock. learned i can live a full life filled with love even if i haven't found someone to share it with. i can find joy in every day even when i'm alone.

i wrote a letter to my future love
put it under a candle
made a wish
six months later i opened it up
read the words aloud
let out a sob
when i realized
i had become everything i wished for

i want love. i want companionship. and that's okay. it will come. but right now, there is no one who appreciates me like i do. no one who can take care of me like i do. no one who notices the little things like i do. there is truly no one who can love me like i do.

if you're hard to find
your person might be too

virgo

[vur-goh]
noun

1. the sixth sign of the zodiac: the mutable earth sign
2. a person born under this sign, usually between august 23 and september 22

clean marble countertops
reapplying sunscreen
saving all your birthday cards
you are enough just as you are
remembering your parents' anniversary
chicken noodle soup
sleeping on it
let me know if you get home safe
pointing out the food between your teeth
battery at 100%
new school shoes
correcting people when they're wrong

virgo

you can only help others
if you help yourself first

whatever you're willing to give
there will always be someone
there to take
and they will
take
take
take
until all you're left with
is resentment

how do i learn and grow
without judging myself

my life is beautiful
but i can only focus
on the spot on the wall

sometimes i wish i could just
take my head off
put it on the bedside table
go through the day
with a little less awareness
find freedom in not having to think
find peace living in my body instead

self pleasure in the bathtub
middle of the day
create holy water
because all that is within you
is divine nectar
holiness greater than this earth
anoint yourself with oil
worship your body whole
your physicality in itself is spiritual
your joy a sacred communion
brush your hair with silver
adorn your fingers with gold
you are a grape from the vine
you are eve's apple
you are not shameful
not guilty
not unclean
you are an otherworldly being

hush little baby
you wrote too many words
momma's gonna buy you
a mirror just like hers

i grew up with conditional love
and frozen food
no wonder nourishment feels abnormal

my mother and i
have different last names
haven't spoken to each other
in two years
but still
we look the same

some days i cannot see
where my mother ends
and i begin

i am her thick hair
her knowing eyes
her grin
before you get the joke

but though i am mother
i am learning to make room
for me too

i am the freckle on my nose
my crooked toe
the way my words
have feelings

i am her
and i am everything she gave up

were you loved
the way you
deserved
to be?

i intend to create a container for myself to be grounded. i give myself healing, loving space. i focus on being in my body, connecting to my body, aligning with my higher self. i give myself space to heal from the traumas of the past. i give myself a blank slate to redefine who i am right now and who i want to become. i treat my body lovingly and with care. i make time and space for whatever comes up for me. this container is one of love and patience. i create a safe place that i can keep coming back to. this is a pause. a reset. a second coming. a becoming. a return to who i truly am. an inspiration for everything i could be.

my vagina is a god
and i pray to mother mary
for every time
i told her she wasn't
convinced god was man
and woman made from rib
but now i know god is a woman
and she lives inside of me

maybe they knew
they were holding
you back

the more i put myself first
the more i can give
and receive unconditional love

♎

libra

[lee-bruh]
noun

1. the seventh sign of the zodiac: the cardinal air sign
2. a person born under this sign, usually between september 23 and october 22

a bubblegum machine
tying a cherry stem with your tongue
knowing all the words to bohemian rhapsody
dreams about flying
polyamory
selective indifference
a lost wedding band
venus riding pegasus
flowers for no reason
justice over loyalty
signing your name perfectly
a magic eight ball

libra

i've never been adulterous
i pinky promise
and my fingers aren't crossed
there's just something
so romantic
about being in love with someone
who has no pressure to reciprocate
your feelings
wait, did i say romantic
i meant pathetic
i've been single for seven years
cause i'm trying to break the pattern
let me love someone with capacity
let me love someone with willingness
let me love someone who wants to love me

pluto moved through my seventh house
tapped venus on the shoulder
whispered,

it's ok to be a hopeless romantic again

why do i start to lose myself
when i think of a future with someone

i hold each part of my body
send the love to it
that i've been withholding
too many years of shame
without touch
wishing my lines and curves
would become straighter
now i'm just
so grateful for this vessel
so happy i get to be here

fall in love but never forget who you are

you were the first person
i liked
like that
in two years
but my anxious
made you avoidant
or maybe it was
the other way around
or maybe no matter what i did
you would always end up saying things
you didn't mean
or maybe no matter what i did
we would never see each other again

not committing might be less scary
giving up might be easier
but if you never put down roots
you will never grow

be love. embrace love in all forms. let go of fear of love. realize love is all you need. create a life full of romance. light candles and incense. wear perfume. buy yourself gifts for no reason. be open to receiving. realize that the only person who can stop you from living your dream is you. and you are deserving of a life worth dreaming about.

thumbnail scratches your shoulder
gently like coming home
like you feel like coming home
my wrist to your lips
feel my pulse in your mouth
always faster than it should be

draped in old flannel
that smells like cedar and sweat
my nose in the pillow
you linger when you're gone
and i'm not afraid to wash the sheets
because you always come back

gentle fingers
part my lips
hold my hand
until my heartbeat slows
and my ears separate from my shoulders

we twist like black liquorice
bitterness escapes from my pores
all i feel with you is sweet
white sheet wraps around me

you pour me water first
and rub my feet after
cause you know i need rest

i'm sorry that your first heartbreak was from someone who was supposed to love you the most. you deserved to feel love as soon as you came to this earth. i'm sorry that the people who were supposed to take care of you couldn't love you in the way you needed. i'm sorry that everyone you've ever loved has hurt you. i'm sorry that you find it hard to love knowing that it always ends in heartbreak. but i hope one day you are loved the way you deserve to be. and i hope one day you can love yourself like that too.

kiss me under the maple tree
i don't wanna be alone anymore
and the moon is full
everyone i know is microdosing psilocybin
but you are a full trip
we finally got our kiddie pool
now you feed me french fries
and talk about the stars like they can hear you
i knew i would fall in love here
i just didn't know where here was

you are the human embodiment of lightning. you don't just light up rooms. you light up the sky. sink into your brightness. it's always there, even when you don't feel it. people feel connected because of you. they feel seen when you're around. you have a magic like no other. it's time to recognize yourself. appreciate the balance that comes naturally to you. it's not ego. you are lightning.

all the love poems i wrote
were about me all along

scorpio

[skawr-pee-oh]
noun

1. the eighth sign of the zodiac: the fixed water sign
2. a person born under this sign, usually between october 23 and november 21

death in disney movies
a tire blown out on the highway
leopard print
cilantro
spiders you let live in your house
sadness from *inside out*
keeping flowers you should throw away
the secret room behind the mirror
cold pizza
smoky quartz
the first snowfall
an upside-down kiss

scorpio

i was in love with a cancer
but never told them
always a little too obsessed with aquarians
capricorns see my heart
but would rather have my stinger
aries drive me wild
leos always taken
sagittarius are for someone else to tame
pisces remind me too much of my brother
virgos, my mother
i loved a taurus so much it almost ended me
made up a whole life with a libra i met once
i'm two-faced enough as a gemini rising
and scorpio on scorpio
baby, that's a crime

sun signs

i'm tired of constantly cracking
myself open
transforming
can't i stay the same
for a little while
can't i just be
this version of me
a little while longer

the crows know
we're the same
suspicious
dining on carcasses
knowing
a sign from god
the last thing you want to see
on your wedding day

i will go to your wedding
in all black
nails and lips painted midnight too
i will shout
i am mourning the loss
of what we could have been
while she cries in white

will you still love me in the winter
when my skin is dry
my lips are chapped
and my smile is less bright
when i sleep in a little longer
and go out a little less
when some days i can't make you laugh
when some days all i do is cry
will you still love me
when some days i don't want to wake up at all

i just wanna flash before your eyes before you die

what do i love more
than building myself up
just to tear myself down again
and become renewed
and become something new

were you turned off
by my boundaries
did i have too many needs
or did you just decide
it was easier being alone

how can i date for fun
when i always end up
in tears

the big things don't make me happy
so i'm trying to find joy in the small
the journey
the day to day
rainbows and tall trees
bea's wiggling bum
karaoke in the car
dance parties in the kitchen
i am trying to hold on
please dear, hold on
but i'm scared of what happens when
i get sick of the day to day
and i just want the journey to end

put my hair in space buns
at my funeral
bury me naked
so i can leave this world
the same way i came in
put my full birth date on my tombstone
i need everyone to know that
scorpios like being underground
and spend their whole lives dying
and being reborn anyway

i am becoming who i am meant to be. who i truly am. i am returning to the original version of self. the version that loves openly without judgment. the version that never heard the harsh words of the world. the version that doesn't hide. in this chapter i am my most authentic being. my voice is brave and loud. i see things clearly without fear or worry. i am truly me.

trust that people have good intentions
be less attached to outcomes
let go of expectations
ask for what you want
surrender to receiving it

sagittarius

[saj-i-tair-ee-uhs]
noun

1. the ninth sign of the zodiac: the mutable fire sign
2. a person born under this sign, usually between
november 22 and december 21

brazilian waxes
finding money in your winter coat
monday hangovers
send nudes
sticky tack
camo print
the opposite of biting your tongue
a last minute road trip
eloping on a weekday
laughing and crying in the same sitting
unrecognized sarcasm
an upside-down roller coaster

sagittarius

i told you i would leave you
without saying i'm sorry
i mean
i never said
i'll leave you
but i changed your shoes
burned your cargo shorts
asked god to forgive us
he said yes
you said no
i just wanted to be a cool girl
sex in the shower girl
i wouldn't have written this five years ago
but now my grandparents
are too old to care
and i don't know where you went
but i'm sure you're somewhere

babe are you ok?
you haven't even touched your existential dread

i am free. of judgment and fear. i see love in everything i do. acceptance. i seek and embrace joy. i realize that this world is filled with love in so many ways. i follow my heart. i do things because they are on my soul path. i do what i truly want. i don't need to care about what other people think.

can this be the last time
i read a birth chart
on a first date

can this be the last time
i admit
i don't talk to my mother

can this be the last time
i pull away
from a first kiss

can this be the last time
i say this is
how much i am

can this be the first time
someone tells me
it's not too much

i have written the first line
of one hundred poems
but then i stop
is it writer's block
or can i say everything
i need to
in six words

i sit with myself
without you

i've been hurt by everyone
who was supposed to
love me unconditionally

no wonder this heart is cracked
no wonder i keep cutting myself
trying to pick up all the pieces

if you keep falling in love
with half-baked people
you will keep feeling the pain
of being loved with half a heart

i am not the cure
for your insecurity
being with me will
only make it worse
i won't save you from your demons
i'll open the door for them
let them sleep in the guest room
i am so sorry i can't fix you
whatever you're running from
will catch up to you
if you're with me

have wine and pastries in a hot bath. fill the water with salt and oil. put on a red dress. take yourself to a wine bar. two glasses of red. fresh sourdough for one. bring your journal and write poems about the waiter. take yourself out for dinner. order a fancy cocktail. get the most expensive thing on the menu. steak frites with truffle fries. dance with each bite. take yourself for a night cap. rejoice when they say there are only seats at the bar. go home full with a new appreciation for you.

i'm still bad at parallel parking
stopped drinking coffee black
cause there's already
a little drummer in my chest
i have eighteen plants
two taller than me
and i still look best in the mornings
sometimes not wearing a thing
i've figured out how to
say what i feel
to cry when someone's not listening
that i can make people dream bigger
just by being honest
if i'm being honest
i don't think of you much anymore
and i hope you're doing ok
but now i know
that people come and go with the seasons
but how they made you feel is there to stay

no self-help books in the winter
if the sun sets at four pm
i don't want to work on me
i want to sleep
escape into a different world
disassociate
it's too cold to improve
it's too dark to see who i'll be next

if you stopped molding yourself to fit into every situation. with every person. in every place you end up. you might realize how loveable you are as you. without adjustments. without considering everyone's feelings but your own. just because you can adapt, doesn't mean you should. you will spend your whole life looking for somewhere you belong if you don't accept yourself first. you don't need to change. you will find people who have room for your wild. just give them a chance to accept the full you.

and at the end
of it all
all you can ask is
was i honest with myself

capricorn

[kap-ri-kawrn]
noun

1. the tenth sign of the zodiac: the cardinal earth sign
2. a person born under this sign, usually between december 22 and january 19

jackets with armpit vents
fresh white sheets
good decisions
a new year's kiss
bone-chilling cold weather
consequences
perfectly wrapped gifts
a plant you can't kill
growing old together
the roman empire
taking it to the grave
talking to trees

capricorn

if the sun is a star
why can't i be one too
instead i feel rock and heavy
not in touch with my emotions
but still ebb and flow with the moon

christmas lights looks sad
on new year's day
especially when you spend it alone
the cold bites colder somehow
even though there isn't any snow
i tried to be optimistic about the year
but couldn't even last a day
can we really get through this again
is there even any other way

i wanna see the other side of saturn
what it looked like when i was born
so i'll stay here in this swaddle
for a little while longer
stork holding me on the lawn
before telling anyone
i never wanted to go inside
in the first place

can i leave now?
saturn's almost done its round
not without casualties
i took a few of its rings on the way
and it took a few chunks out of me
now i am made of craters
now i am the moon

i liked that you had an ipod
plugged permanently in your car
cherry wine or *take me to church*
i can still hear you tap along

i liked that you charmed waiters
and were a good tipper
and most of the time
i liked when you drove fast

i liked the curls
on the top of your head
that you picked out outfits
the night before

but your sheets always felt like
they were falling off your bed
and i could never sleep
through the night with you

i wonder if my unconscious knew
that even though
i liked all these things
i wasn't falling in love with you

how do you start a relationship
without seeing it end
in your head first

i started holding other people
to the standards i hold myself to

turns out no one could meet them either

did
you hear
me when i
said i feared
intimacy?

remember when
you slept in all day
i wanted to get up early
but was trying to be the cool girl

went for brunch late
no more smoked salmon
you asked me what
i didn't like about you

i felt like you were asking
for it to be over
or maybe i was asking
for it to be over

and though i don't remember
what i told you
i remember you said
i shut down sometimes
so i shut you out instead

i'm learning to stop putting people
on pedestals
cause when they fall
i'm the one who breaks

i wanna kiss you on new years
promise you won't
disappear at midnight

i want to be a tree
so tall i can see what's next
i want to be a leaf
so i can fall without fearing
where i'll land
i'd love to be a branch
to explore my possibilities
always know that i can grow
in different directions
i want to be the best version of me
and i think that might be a tree

i do not have to give all of myself
to get what i want

maybe i'll spend my whole life
finding love
not just once
but every day
in places i never expected

i no longer have people in my life who do not do what they say they are going to do. i am done with checking in. i am done with reminders. i no longer take on the mental exhaustion that comes with being reliable for another person. i call in self-sufficiency. i call in reliability. i call in competency, consistency, the ability to follow through. all of my connections are filled with ease. we are responsible for ourselves and we benefit from a mutual, natural ebb and flow.

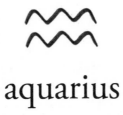

aquarius

[uh-kwair-ee-uhs]
noun

1. the eleventh sign of the zodiac: the fixed air sign
2. a person born under this sign, usually between january 20 and february 18

unicorns
forgetting to reply
snowflakes
a one-way ticket
intellectualizing your feelings
light-up sneakers
a tote bag bursting at the seams
knowing better
just five more minutes
bear hugs
a god complex
bending the rules

aquarius

my love for you lasted the longest
but it was also the saddest
i wish competency
wasn't such a turn on
i wish it wasn't so easy
to romanticize someone
i could never be with
i wish i was satisfied
with just friends
but if i'm being honest
i wasn't
i wish i could be happy
for your wife and kids
but if i'm being honest
i'm not
but most of all
i wish it didn't take all this time to realize

i was too in love with you for far too long

i will be alone this winter
sorry if i gave you the wrong impression
but my heart isn't warm enough
to keep either of us alive

i know the earth isn't flat
but it feels like it stopped turning
i am tired of processing
what i cannot comprehend
i keep searching for answers
but thinking doesn't help
when everything is out of your control

i'd like to have a word with whoever
started a pasta sauce company
with your name
i'm just trying to make dinner
but you're everywhere
i'm just trying to be alone
but you're everywhere

i held on to
my washing machine
spinning uncontrollably
closed my eyes and
asked if i could skip ahead two years
it's not that i don't want to live
it's that i don't want to live right now
i want to see the next part
so i know this part is worth it

thank you for teaching me unconditional love. for having the best sense of humour. for bringing light into every room. for having a deep understanding of me as a person and always holding space for who i am. thank you for catharsis through cooking, for welcoming me into your kitchen. for supporting me, for always paying special attention to me. you showed me how to be brave and strong, and that brave and strong can come in any package. i wish you felt less pressure to hold it all together. i wish you were able to find yourself more. thank you for instilling core values in me. and thank you for watching over me now.

te quiero

dear nana III

what if death does not mean
you have lost someone forever
what if it means

you have an abundance of love to come

i will be the last woman
in my family
to be used as a pin cushion
a mirror
a reflection of a man's wounds

i took a thread
promised it i would get better
weaved it between my two front teeth
gagged it down
swallowed till it reached my stomach
i can suture one hundred years
of open wounds
women bleeding from the inside
a family of good girls
the more i speak
the more they hear
the more i heal
the more pain becomes love

it ends with me

maybe everything dark
has something to show you

maybe the absence of light
does not mean hope is lost

maybe it's an invitation
to let your light shine brighter

maybe it's trying to show you
that you have stardust at your fingertips

maybe everything you touch will turn to gold

i've been shining for others
for so long that
i forgot what it felt like
to shine for myself

the star

i am ready to put down the axe
the forest is empty
i am letting go of
the fear of being let go of
cause it only leads to people
who don't have the capacity
for my love
i am planting a new seed
i am ready to meet the person
who can love me equally

i kept dating people that were living in a way that was less than what i wanted. and i didn't really know why. i couldn't figure it out. if i had high standards, how did they fall so easily. but if this was a pattern, the only common denominator was me. i realized that my fear of being left was getting in the way of being with people who could meet me where i'm at. i was settling for less in the hopes of fun, in the hopes of a connection with potential, but by abandoning what i really wanted, my fear became a self-fulfilling prophecy. everyone i lowered my standards for ended up leaving anyway. maybe they felt they weren't what i wanted. maybe chasing after people who aren't your equal makes them feel like they're not enough. but it all came back to me. not choosing myself. when i choose myself, i choose people who also choose themselves. i choose people who have the capacity for overflowing, unconditional love. i choose people who see the big me, see my capacity, and don't run from it. i choose people who see all this space i take up and say, me too.

i shone a light on all the cracks
in my foundation
fell to the ground
when i realized
what was holding me up
was holding me back
now that i have nothing but earth
i can plant seeds just for me
now that i've met my shadows
i can grow from a place of love instead

pisces

[pis-eez]
noun

1. the twelfth sign of the zodiac: the mutable water sign
2. a person born under this sign, usually between february 19 and march 20

the last cupcake
butterfly clips
a seahorse
finding money on the ground
bottomless mimosas
romanticizing your life
a cloud with a rainbow coming out of it
forgetting what you want to remember
remembering what you want to forget
periwinkle
hurting people you love by accident
losing your boarding pass

pisces

why can't you be
the version of you
that goes deeper than the ocean
the real you is a puddle
come dream with me
the you i made up
is so much better
i think you'd like them
come dream with me
breathe underwater
i'll give you gills
and you'll be everything
i ever wanted you to be

i'm afraid i'll disappear
if i close my eyes

at least you taught me
that i wasn't going to find self worth
through intimacy

there's so much to
be sad about
when you're trying
to fall in love

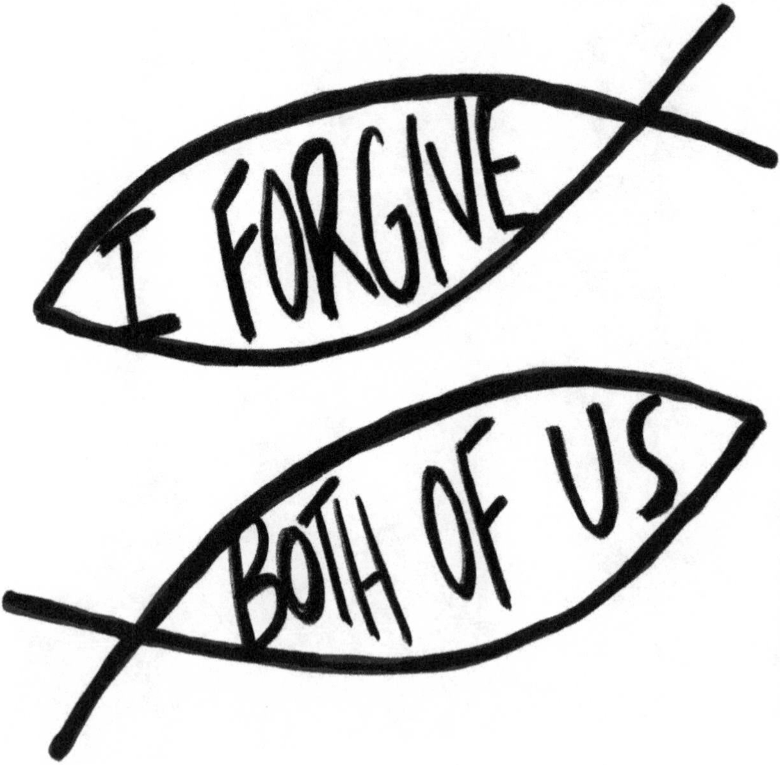
I FORGIVE
BOTH OF US

one day it will
finally feel
like it's in the past

i want to be a sailboat
without a captain
less control
more moving with the waves
trusting that water flows its way
for a reason
that it will carry me
where i need to be next

you can hold the ocean in your hands. even if no one else believes it. your intuition is a gift. stop second guessing yourself. when you feel lost, find water. a stream, a river, a lake. a bathtub will do, too. connect with its frequency. cry if you need to. your tears are magic. sometimes you have to give up the dream of feeling understood. your current may flow in different ways, but you will always belong here.

what if i'm not a sad girl anymore
what if i'm the happiest i've ever been

i'm moving to an island
hiring a personal chef
to make me mushroom fettuccine
put a bellini on my bedside
before i wake up

i'm moving to an island
getting a tan
letting my feet stay sandy
taking a lover
staining white sheets

i'm moving to an island
swimming with the dolphins
getting a starfish tattoo
with a meaning
i'll forget

i'm moving to an island
falling in love
with every sunset
putting letters in a bottle
that you'll never get to read

after all this time
i have to be close
to love

i am finding happiness
and learning how to sit
in the moment and feel it

poetry is a full moon you cannot see. it's ducks swimming under a bridge. it's the last piece of halloween candy. it's the first time you break your own heart. it's the way blowing out a candle fills your nose. poetry is a broken nail. an unfinished book. a ring lost in the lake. poetry is not proud. it does not judge. it finds the truth and sets it on fire. poetry has no expectations. you cannot let a poem down. poetry is a deep breath. poetry sees you for who you really are, and says welcome home.

when you feel too external
go inside yourself
joy, freedom and
unconditional love reside there

acknowledgements

thank you to anyone who has ever purchased one of my books, bought one for a friend, or let a friend borrow a copy. thank you for your sweet messages on instagram, for your heartfelt comments on tiktok, for letting my words into your heart and for sharing them with people you love. we've really created a lovefest together and i wouldn't be able to reach so many people who feel the same feels without you.

thanks dad for being my favourite cancer and for going on this healing journey with me. thanks bri for being my favourite aquarius, the ultimate hype girl and probably the first person to share and love this book other than me. it is such a blessing to have a friend who sees your vision and believes in your dreams as much as you. thanks chinye for being my favourite virgo, for being here since book one, for letting me ship proofs to you when they won't ship them to canada, and for loving and supporting me for ten whole years. thanks oma and nana for being the best taurus-aquarius duo and grandmas a girl could ask for. i am so proud to be your granddaughter and it was such a privilege to be around your love for each other.

and thanks to me, my favourite scorpio, for formatting, editing, illustrating and publishing this book all by myself. we did it!

about the author

michaela angemeer is passionate about sharing her self love journey and inspiring readers to spend more time with their feelings. she's a canadian poet who was born on november 18th, 1992 at 6:37 pm in brampton, ontario.

after sharing her poetry on instagram for a year, michaela self-published her first collection of poetry, *when he leaves you*, in 2018. the book debuted as the #1 new release in canadian poetry online. her second book, *you'll come back to yourself*, was released in 2019, making it to the #1 best seller in poetry the following year. her third collection, *please love me at my worst*, became the #1 best seller in poetry shortly after its release in 2020.

michaela's newest book, *poems for the signs*, is a heartfelt exploration of the twelve zodiac signs. it's a collection about looking for love, self-reflection, depression, healing ancestral patterns, and finding beauty in being alone.

michaela now lives in kitchener, ontario with her frenchton, bea. you can find her at local coffee shops, her favourtie wine bar, or in her backyard looking up at the moon.

get in touch on tiktok & instagram: @michaelapoetry
michaelapoetry.com

CPSIA information can be obtained
at www.ICGtesting.com
Printed in the USA
LVHW100252180822
726267LV00006B/341